cloverleaf books™

Holidays and Special Days

Emma's Easter

Lisa Bullard

illustrated by **Constanza Basaluzzo**

M MILLBROOK PRESS · MINNEAPOLIS

For Laura —L.B.
For Julia . . . the reason of my life —C.B.

Millbrook Press
A division of Lerner Publishing Group, Inc.
241 First Avenue North
Minneapolis, MN 55401 USA

For reading levels and more information, look up this title at
www.lernerbooks.com.

Main body text set in Slappy Inline 18/28.
Typeface provided by T26.

Library of Congress Cataloging-in-Publication Data

Bullard, Lisa.
     Emma's Easter / by Lisa Bullard ; illustrated by Constanza
Basaluzzo.
         p.   cm. — (Cloverleaf books. Holidays and special days)
     Includes index.
     ISBN 978-0-7613-5080-4 (lib. bdg. : alk. paper)
     ISBN 978-0-7613-8840-1 (EB pdf)
     1. Easter. I. Basaluzzo, Constanza. II. Title.
GT4935.B85 2012
394.2667—dc23   2011022229

Manufactured in the United States of America
2 - 41199 - 10791 - 3/17/2017

TABLE OF CONTENTS

Do you know what day it is tomorrow? It's **Easter!** We get ready by decorating eggs. We dye them the colors of **Spring flowers.**

Easter is a spring celebration. It is always on a Sunday.

See how I wrote my name on this one?

Chapter Two
Easter Morning

I'm so **"egg-cited"** that I can hardly sleep.
Finally, it's Easter morning. And guess what?

Some German settlers came to the United States about three hundred years ago. They seem to have brought the Easter Bunny with them! The settlers' children found eggs from the bunny on Easter morning. U.S. kids have looked forward to Easter ever since.

The **Easter Bunny** left us baskets of candy. Jelly beans are my favorite!

The Easter Bunny also **hid our eggs** all over the house. We hunt everywhere for them.

The U.S. president has an Easter egg roll every year. It takes place on the Monday after Easter. Families come to the White House from all over the country. They roll eggs with spoons and do other fun things.

I find an egg in the bathtub.

There's even one in Scout's bowl.

But I **can't find** my "Emma" egg anywhere.

Finally, Mom says I need to get ready for **church**. There's an egg in my shiny new shoes. There's an egg in my fancy **Easter hat**.

Easter is a church holiday for Christians. But it's a special day for other people too. They are happy about the new life that comes with spring.

15

Chapter Four

Where's That Egg?

After church, the whole family comes to our house. My relatives all bring food for Easter dinner.

And **Grandma** has made lots of **kulich**. That's a sweet Easter bread. Grandma says it's from Russia.

Many different countries have their own special Easter breads. People in England eat hot cross buns at Easter time.

17

Finally, our bellies are stuffed. Then we all look for my "Emma" egg. We can't find it anywhere! Grandpa says maybe Scout ate it for his Easter dinner.

Mom sends me to bed after everyone goes home. She says egg hunting will have to wait until tomorrow. Then—can you guess what I found under my covers?

That Easter Bunny sure is tricky!

Make Your Own Easter Flowers

Easter is a time for beautiful spring flowers to bloom.
Now you can make flowers to decorate your Easter table.

What you will need:

white and green construction paper

straws, as many as the number of flowers you want to make

stapler

tape

scissors

pencil

1) Lay your nonwriting hand flat on the white paper. Spread out your fingers and thumb. Trace the outline of your hand in pencil.

2) Draw some leaves on the green paper.
   Make them about 3 inches long.

3) Cut out the tracing of your hand and the leaves.

4) Curl the fingers of the handprint around a pencil.

5) Twist the bottom of the handprint into a cone shape.
   The fingers should curl outward.

6) Tape the cone together.

7) Staple the bottom of the cone to a straw.

8) Staple one leaf about halfway down the straw. Staple a second leaf below that, on the other side of the straw.

9) You have made your first flower. Make as many more as you want to.

10) Place your flowers in a vase for your Easter dinner table.
    Or put one next to each dinner plate as a decoration.

GLOSSARY

celebration: doing something to show how special or important a day is

Christianity: a religion that follows the life and teachings of Jesus

decorating: adding things to something to make it look pretty

Easter: a holiday from the Christian religion that celebrates Jesus rising from the dead

fancy: extra special or with lots of decorations

favorite: the one you like the most

kulich: a sweet Easter bread that is common in Russia

religion: a set of beliefs in a god or gods

settler: a person who goes to live in a new country

BOOKS

Anderson, Sheila. *Are You Ready for Spring?* Minneapolis: Lerner Publications Company, 2010.
What happens in spring besides Easter? Read this book to find out.

Knudsen, Shannon. *Easter around the World.* Minneapolis: Millbrook Press, 2005.
This book shows how people celebrate Easter in many different countries.

O'Neal, Debbie Trafton. *J Is for Jesus: An Easter Alphabet and Activity Book.*
Minneapolis: Augsburg Fortress, 2006.
This book talks more about Easter as a church holiday. It also includes crafts and activities.

WEBSITES

Cracking Eggs
http://www.crackingeggs.co.uk/index.php
This website from the British Egg Information Service brings you lots of egg puzzles, fun, and facts.

LERNER *e* SOURCE™
Expand learning beyond the printed book. Download free, complementary educational resources for this book from our website, www.lerneresource.com.

Easter Egg-tivities
http://www.meddybemps.com/easter/index.html
This website from Chateau Meddybemps gives you a chance to read an Easter story and play.

Easter Games
The White House Easter Egg Roll
http://www.whitehouse.gov/photos-and-video/photogallery/white-house-easter-egg-roll
This photo gallery from the U.S. government shows the 2010 White House Easter Egg Roll.

INDEX